FUN and FUNDAMENTALS

activities
for the
classroom

FUN and FUNDAMENTALS

activities
for the
classroom

Margaret E.T. Noyes, EdD

ACADEMIC THERAPY PUBLICATIONS
SAN RAFAEL, CALIFORNIA

Academic Therapy Publications
P.O. Box 899, 1539 Fourth Street
San Rafael, California 94901

Tests, books, and materials
for and about the learning disabled

International Standard Book Number:
0-87879-179-5

Illustrations: Margaret E. Noyes

Contents

Acknowledgments

This book has developed from the expressed need of teachers to have activities for enrichment of individuals and groups in special classes and/or resource situations.

Ideas given here can be adapted by teachers to meet many situations. Many of the activities are new; some are old favorites which have been brought up to date or modified.

Contributions to this booklet were made by graduate students at Texas Woman's University: Betty Bender, Karen Bretches, James Dean, Bonita Gillespie, Frances Hamby, Brenda Hauk, Martin Hearne, Patsy Hussy, Jeanette Knippel, Gene Lane, Mary Mahon, Mary Murray, Victoria Overpeck, Patricia Ownby, Judy Pomerenke, Marsha Ramey, Susan Read, Betty Stoker, Billy Jo Wood.

CHAPTER 1

Classroom Management

Classroom Atmosphere: The comfort of the classroom can govern the children's reactions. Temperature and humidity should be considered. Temperatures should range between 68 and 70 degrees Fahrenheit. Humidity should be between 40 and 60 percent. If a child is hyperactive, a slightly increased temperature has a tendency to slow him down. If a child is sluggish, a slightly lower temperature has a tendency to perk him up.

Rules: When a child is required to do a certain thing or task, this becomes a rule.

    1. Be sure the rule is well defined.

    2. Be sure the rule is reasonable.

    3. Be sure the rule is enforceable.

Rules alone do very little to influence behavior; they must be made effective and important by providing reinforcement for appropriate behavior.

Reinforcement: Reinforcement should be immediate! The point system may be used for positive or negative reinforcement. Points may be given to or taken away from children for:

    1. Coming into the room, being seated, and getting ready for work.

    2. Completing a task.

    3. Working diligently for a given period of time.

Reinforcers that teach new behaviors are:

1. Verbal.
2. Liquid and food items.
3. Tokens, chips, stars, play money (or real, which may well be the least expensive!) to purchase other reinforcers, such as field trips, candy, toys, books, or trips to the game room.

Immediate exchange of tokens is good for current reinforcement.

Vary the number of tokens for different situations and be sure that the child understands the system. A chart could be used to explain the value of the tokens and the work needed to earn them.

Reinforce the child frequently when teaching a new skill.

Rap: Rap or discussion sessions are helpful. Children should be urged to:

1. Ask questions and talk about things that bother them.
2. Come up with several possible solutions to the problem and then evaluate each of them.

Manipulation on the part of the teacher should lead to a more profitable discussion from which the children will learn:

1. Not to interrupt when someone else is talking.
2. Not to be overly critical of someone's point of view.
3. To realize that sometimes there is more than one correct answer to a question.

Why: Make *why* the motive power. Encourage the children to bring their "whys" to school.

Library Center: Set up a section of the room to be very attractive and flexible—something new from time to time: fresh pictures on the bulletin board, a new book open to an interesting page, or a fresh bunch of flowers on the table.

Play Center: Children can play-act many interesting functions. This is good for developing oral language ability. Several students may do this without the aid of a teacher. Play-acting develops the experience of working and playing together.

Guest Speakers: Use as many people in the community as are willing to help. Be sure to clear the asking of an outsider with the administration first. Suggestions:

1. Transportation company employees can "give" the students many trips. Slides, picture brochures, road maps, and many other aids could be used.

2. War veterans or members of nonpartisan patriotic groups could speak to them on patriotism, and how important it is to be a good citizen.

3. Athletes can share their roles, or former roles, in a certain sport and stress the importance of sportsmanship and teamwork.

4. Newspaper reporters could do a story for the local newspaper about something the class is doing. After the story appears in print, the reporter could come to the class and explain briefly what is involved in getting a story in the paper.

5. Service people: Policemen, bakers, firemen, retail merchants, doctors, school personnel, can explain their function in the community.

Making Friends: Do not let your children limit their acquaintances to your classroom. Ask other groups or classes to visit your class when possible. Attend as many school plays, concerts, pep rallys, ball games, assemblies, and other activities as possible. Let the children discuss how they can become acquainted with new people. Let them practice introducing themselves to each other in various ways and situations which may be suggested by the teacher.

Leadership Responsibilities: Select different children each day, week, month, or semester, depending on the job to be done, to be "teacher's assistant." All children should be given the opportunity to participate at some time.

Make a chart with the student's name and the job to be done. Be sure to put a check or star next to the child's name when the task is completed. Children like to see and hear their names. Some jobs to be done:

1. Attendance check
2. Help with opening exercises
3. Distributing and collecting materials
4. Greeting and introducing guests
5. Cleaning the blackboards
6. Keeping the room neat and in order
7. Helping make daily schedules

Always allow the children to do any of the jobs they can do, even though you can do them better and faster.

Special Days: Type the name of each month on an index card. Make a section for special days or weeks to be observed at school. Special ideas for bulletin boards may be included.

Ideas: Set aside a period sometime during the week for doing something different: taking a walk, playing folk games, or writing riddles. The children will like the element of surprise.

Calendars: Save your old calendars. Pictures and numbers have many uses.

Blocks: Children with poor coordination may try using blocks with pictures, words, or numbers attached. Children with poor speech can pick up blocks in answer to questions. Large blocks may be made out of foam rubber.

Coveralls: Old shirts buttoned down the back make good coveralls for the children to wear when painting. Leave the sleeves on, as they give further protection.

Acting: Acting out imaginary situations sometimes helps children to make the right decision.

Voice: To get the classroom quiet, lower your voice to a whisper and call on a child to answer your question. Children will begin listening for their names to be called.

Clutter: If the books, pencils, and paper are scattered about the room, try this: collect all the items and hold them for ransom. Let each item out of place have a price. For example, to get a lost notebook back, the child may have to clean the chalkboard erasers. The children will soon learn to keep their things in place, and the room will be neater and cleaner.

Bulletin Board: If the bulletin board space is small, place a strip of cloth underneath the chalkboard and windows. Many drawings can be pinned to this strip of cloth.

Window shades hung at the top of your chalkboard give added space when you need it for charts, number combinations, color words. Vinyl-covered ones can be cleaned more easily than paper shades.

Lunch Money: Primary children can be helped to bring their lunch money on the right day by a colored tag which says, "Lunch money—tomorrow."

Assigning Duties: A good method of assigning room duties is the old grab bag. Write duties on slips of paper, put them in the bag, and have each pupil close his eyes and select one. This will be his duty for the day.

Settling Down: The teacher can start a countdown: 10, 9, 8, 7, and so on. The slow ones may have to be helped sometimes by using 2½, 2, 1½, 1, near the end.

Turning out the light for a few moments can help settle the children.

Quiet time can be timed by letting the children watch the grains of sand fall to the bottom of an egg timer.

E-Z Flannel Board: Put outing flannel on a board. A child can spend worthwhile time working with various materials such as matching rhyming words, story-telling pictures, numbers. Small strips of sandpaper on the backs of pictures or cards work very well and are easy to fix. A piece of flannel glued to the back of the cards will also work.

Disciplinary Action:

1. If a child is disturbing others, write him a note instead of correcting him orally.

2. If a child *must* talk out, give him a magic slate and let him *write* instead.

3. Deprivation of privileges is an effective method of discipline.

4. When a child misbehaves, negative attention might reinforce his behavior. *Try ignoring him.*

5. Isolation and reinforcement can be used to alter behavior.

Time: Make signs to represent a designated period of time. Use a different color for each time for those who cannot read.

The Distractibles: Assign a special study area to a child who is easily disturbed by others. This can be referred to as his "office." Packing boxes, file cabinets, bookcases, and other classroom furniture can be used to make study areas.

CHAPTER 2

Arithmetic

Number Sequence: Use connect-the-dot pictures to help children learn the numbers in sequence. With older children the same pictures can be adapted to counting by twos, fives, etc. by changing the numbers. These pictures can also be used with a unit on money. Make each dot equal to a dime or a quarter so the student has to add to get the proper sequence. Suggest buying dot-to-dot books and adapting to arithmetic needs.

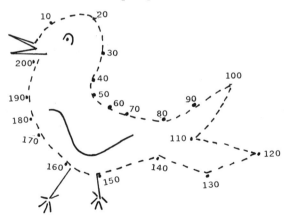

Bean Bag Game: On large poster board mark off 9 or 16 squares and write the numbers in the areas. Put this chart on the floor and have a small number of children take turns placing a bean bag on it. As the bean bag lands on a number the child placing it must call out that number within a specified number of seconds. This will help young children with immediate recognition of the numbers. As they become more advanced, other charts with larger numbers, various mathematical signs, or even problems may be used.

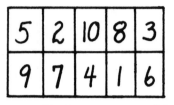

Counting Exercises: Find as many small bottles (babyfood jars, prescription bottles) as possible, and write numbers on them. Fill each jar with the number of dried beans corresponding to the number on the jar. The child can then take the beans out of the jar, count them, and check to see if the number he comes up with corresponds to the number written on the jar. The exercise can then be reversed. The child must fill the empty jars with the correct number of beans.

Egg Carton Uses: Buy 12 ping-pong balls and number them with a magic marker from 1 to 12. Put them in the egg carton to help teach the concept of a dozen and half dozen.

Put the odd numbered balls across the top and the even numbered ones along the bottom to concretely illustrate the set of odd or even numbers from 1 to 12. This also helps teach counting by twos.

Number Puzzles: Write numbers from 1 to 10 on construction paper, then cut into puzzles for child to work. The paper may be laminated for longer wear. Teachers can make specific numbers for children having difficulty, particularly with reversals.

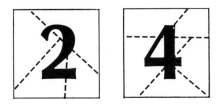

Matching Shapes: A domino game can be made very cheaply from one-inch by two-inch boards (easily picked up around construction sites) cut into four-inch lengths. Paint each board a bright color. Then paint a geometric shape on each half. Have the children play a game similar to dominoes, but matching shapes instead of numbers.

Shapes: Use a deck of cards to teach sequence, shapes. Play games similar to "21" that involve counting and adding to a given number.

Simple Problems: Color by number coloring books can be used for practice in solving simple problems. For example, change the numbers in the coloring books to problems that equal that number. All the areas that are numbered four can be changed to problems whose answers are 4—8 - 4, 2 + 2, 6 - 2, 3 + 1, etc. The child must solve the problem before he can look on the key to find out what color the area should be *colored.*

Coverall Contest: Cut basic shapes from felt (circles, triangle, square, rectangle, etc.) in various sizes and in two different colors. The two different colored figures should correspond in shape and size. Set up a flannel board with two different colored sides in the front of the room. Cards are prepared with the names of the shapes on them. Choose two teams. One member of each team draws a card which names the figure he must pick from his team's color. The child then puts the shape on the flannel board. In alternate turns, the boys and girls draw cards with instructions and put the shapes on the board. The team that can put the most shapes on the board without overlapping them is the winner.

Bingo Game: Make cards like Bingo cards but put numbers in the squares instead of letters. The caller has cards with problems on them which he calls out. The player must put his marker on the number that is the answer to that problem. Example: The caller says "6 + 2," and the player must put his marker on "8." For longer life of Bingo cards, make them out of tagboard and laminate them.

Time Glasses: Make frames for eye glasses from Mason jar lids or any other circular object and ear pieces from pipe cleaners. Cut circles from poster board to fit inside the lids. Make 12 circles with the time written on them. Example: 1:00. Make another 12 circles with a clock face showing the times. Scramble and have the child match the time with the picture by putting them in the frames. As the child progresses, have him match half hour and quarter hour.

Ping-Pong Problems: Write problems on ping-pong balls. Throw them up in the air. The child that catches the ball may answer the problem to gain a point. This may be a running game, and the child who has the greatest number of points on his chart by the end of the week will be awarded a prize.

Relay Race: Children make two lines. Have flash cards prepared and in two separate stacks. The first two people in line pick up a card, then run to the chalkboard, and write the answer to the problem on the board. If correct, the team gains one point. If incorrect, the team loses one point.

Shape Game (circle, triangle, square, rectangle, etc.): Use two teams, all players being blindfolded. Have the shapes made from paper or wood. Hand identical shapes to the first two people in line. The first to name the shape moves his team up one space.

Dice: From cubes of wood or commercial soft foam make a large set of dice. Paint the dots on them in bright colors. The children throw the dice and make a problem out of the number combination that comes up. For example, if a two and a three come up, the problem could be either two plus three, three minus two, or—for more advanced children—two times three.

Coins: In conjunction with studying money, the concepts of more, less, and equal can be strengthened by passing out coins to the class. Have the children compare their coins with those of their neighbors', telling if theirs is more than, less than, or equal to their neighbors', and how much difference there is. These concepts could be taught by means of a race of the teacher wishes, or partners could see how many points they could accumulate by using the right words.

Carpet Squares: Get carpet samples; print numbers from 1 to 20 on them (with a felt-tip pen); and put them in sequence on the floor. Tell children to stand on a specific number. Later tell them to stand on the number before "6," etc. Still later, put the numbered squares out of sequence and have the children find the correct numbers.

Shoe Box: Cut a slit along top of lid for holding a series of numbers, colors, or shapes. Cut holes in the lid close to the numbers. Children are given pictures of objects to match to numbers. They can also match words to numbers (*1* to *one*, etc.)

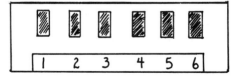

Math Treasure Hunt: Make a game path with numerals in the various squares, along with an operational sign. The answer at end of trail opens treasure box number 5. "Treasures" could be tokens, free time for a game, etc. Adapt math problems to the child's specific needs.

CHAPTER 3

Reading and Language

Finish the Story: Collect large, interesting action pictures. Tell the beginning of a story to which one of the pictures supplies a plausible ending. The child listens to the teacher's story, selects a picture to complete the story, then tells how the story ended.

Shapes the Thing: Give each pupil an envelope with cut-out shapes corresponding to those on the work sheet. Prepare brightly colored construction shapes beforehand. Have the pupil paste his cut-out shapes where they fit. Variations:

    1. Match word shapes just as with the shapes.

    2. Match the words.

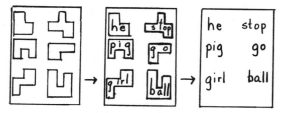

Fish: Cut out fish from cardboard or tagboard. Put a paper clip on each fish. Use a dowel, string, and a magnet to make the fishing pole. Write simple letters, words, etc. on the fish. If the child reads the words correctly, he may keep the fish until the end of the game. To make the game more fun, decorate a cardboard box with a bright underwater scene.

Weather Man: Make from felt weather shapes such as an umbrella, clouds, sun, snowman, raindrops, etc. (A pre-made set can be purchased but will need additional parts.) Make weather words, including school days, using felt and a felt-tip pen. Each school day let a different child be the weather man. He selects the cutouts and words best corresponding to the day's weather. To take this another step, make cut-outs of a child and clothing. Then, the child must also select the proper clothing for the day.

Word Puzzles: Start with the child's name, then progress on to other words. Take tagboard or any heavy paper and write the word in large letters with a felt-tip pen. Cut the word into two pieces to make the puzzle. As skills improve, the puzzles can be cut accordingly.

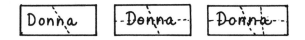

Word Lotto: Use large picture cards made from tagboard composed of a number of different pictures cut from magazines with the word written under the picture. As a word is called, it is covered with a small duplicate card. The first child covering all the words on his card wins. Later the same game can be played using just the words.

Ping-Pong Words: Write the children's names on ping-pong balls and place in a basket. The children take turns drawing a ball from the basket and identifying the child whose name is on the ball. The words may be written on plastic tape or masking tape in order to make the balls reusable. Variations:

    1. Write simple functional words on the balls.
    2. Write simple words on the balls. The child names rhyming words.

Hide and Seek: Divide the class into small groups. Place a number of instructions on pieces of paper in a container. Each group selects an instruction and proceeds as directed. "Go to the teacher's desk. Look in the green book. What is on the red paper?" A picture of some animal, flower, or object may be there. The first group answering their question wins the point.

Silly Sayings: Slips of paper with "silly sayings" are placed in a paper sack. Each child draws a slip for the antics he is to perform. For example: "Blow your nose and brush your teeth." "Sing a song and shake your head."

Grocery Store: Set up a small grocery store using empty containers of familiar products: milk, cereal, canned goods, etc. The children take turns being the shopkeeper and the customer. The teacher tells the customer an item to purchase from the store. The number of items can be gradually increased as the students become more proficient. The customer goes shopping and names the products he wishes to purchase. The shopkeeper then selects the items from the shelves.

Cross the River: Words are printed on pieces of cardboard and placed on the floor as if they were stepping stones crossing the river. This may be done with two sets of stones and using two teams to see which team gets to the other side first. As the teacher flashes the words written on flash cards, the first team answering correctly may advance to the next stone. If a player answers incorrectly, he "falls in the river" and must go back one stone.

Circle of Words: Construct a large circle of cardboard with a smaller circle (approximately one-third the size of the larger circle) attached by a brad in the center. Divide each circle into eight sections. Glue familiar pictures cut from magazines and coloring books on the edges of the larger circle. Write the name for each of the pictures in a section on the smaller circle. The child turns the "word circle" to match the "picture circle." Variations:

    1. Alternate small circles may be made substituting beginning letters, rhyming words, or pictures.

    2. The words or letters may be written on the small circle and the child draws one or more pictures to match; or he draws pictures of rhyming words.

Sew a Match: Draw or glue pictures in two columns on tagboard. These may represent either rhyming words or beginning sounds. Use a hole punch to make holes beside each picture. The child selects a color of yarn and laces the yarn to the appropriate matching picture. He may use a different color of yarn for each match.

Christmas Story: A Christmas tree may be drawn on cardboard decorated with designs representing ornaments. The child writes as many "Christmas words" on the ornaments as possible. This may be varied according to special days during the year: hearts for Valentine's Day, eggs and bunnies for Easter; turkey's tail feathers for Thanksgiving.

Wild West: The shape of a cowboy is drawn on cardboard and placed on the chalkboard. On one side of the figure the first parts of compound words are written. The second parts are written on the other side. Two teams are formed from the class to represent a blue team and a red team. Each team is given a set of colored string attached between two thumbtacks. In alternating turns the players go to the board and match the words using the string. A specified amount of time should be allowed for a turn. If a match has not been made during the time limit, the turn passes to the other team. When all the children have had a chance to play, the two colors are counted to determine which team has won. Variations:

1. Rhyming words, words and beginning letters, duplicate words may even be used for inexperienced readers.
2. The figures and words may be varied according to the units being studied: community helpers, Indians, animals, etc.

Finish My Story: This is a game to help the students hear consonants and is also good to help them remember word sequences. The first child would start the game by saying, "I am going to the dime store and I'm going to buy a dump truck." The next child must say "dump truck" and add a new word. The next child must repeat these two words and add a third new word. The teacher may have to help some of the students with the word sequence and finding their own new word. The store can be changed to other types of stores, or might be "going to a party" or "going to a picnic," and children tell what they will wear or what they will take with them. During the game, new initial consonants are added frequently.

What's My Word?: This game provides review of special words that the children are using in reading. Pass out cards with one word per card to all the children except one. The teacher calls out words. As soon as each child knows his word, he holds up his card. When all the cards are in sight, the teacher pronounces one of the words held up by the children. The child with no card tries to find the word. If he finds the word, he may say the word and take the word to his chair. The child who now has no card is "it" and the game starts again.

Fits to a Letter: A large letter is made, generally from 12 to 14 inches. Each team is given one of these letters, and all the children are given pencils. The team that can furnish the most words for a letter is the winner. This activity could also be done on an individual basis with a child doing a letter at his seat. He could do this when he finishes his other work early.

Playing Cards: This game can be played with nouns or verbs. A number of cards are made with a word on one side and the illustration on the back. The cards are put into a stack with Side 1 showing. As the child takes the card and says the word, he checks the back to be sure if he was correct. If correct, he gets a point, if not, he must put it back on the bottom of the stack and start again. This game can be adapted for group play, also using teams and keeping score for each team.

Where's the Ending: Make up cards that have base words such as *use, help, kind,* etc. Make up other cards that have suffixes on them such as *ful, ness, less,* etc. The child must match them and write them down. He works until he is able to match them all. This game could be adapted for groups with teams. Another way might be to make several suffix cards and put them in a stack. Three or four children can play. Each child would have four or five base words. The children would take turns. A child would draw a suffix card. If he can match it to his base card, he would set it aside, if he could not, he would put the suffix card back under the stack. The child that finishes matching all his base cards first is the winner.

Picture Dictionary: Two cards would be made. One is called a dictionary card. The other is the card that the child will need to find the word to match the picture. The dictionary card will help the child to see if he made the correct choice. He needs to be cautioned not to rely too much on the dictionary card. At the beginning, maybe only two will be given and as the child progresses, more words at a time will be added.

Picture-Word Puzzles: These may be made by drawing or using a magazine picture on one side of a card and printing the word on the other section. When cut, the pieces will only fit if they are matched correctly.

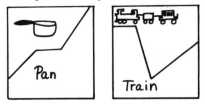

Alphabet Book: An ABC book can be made with a different letter on each page and a magazine or self-drawn picture on the same page. The picture will help to indicate the sound.

School Map: For reading readiness, a large map of the school can be drawn with children helping to locate and draw on the map such locations as the classroom, lunchroom, water fountains, exits, and entrances.

Alphabet File: Make a file using a shoe box and envelopes. Cut small squares from tagboard or construction paper. Make several for each letter of the alphabet. Sort them according to letters and put them in envelopes. Let children choose letters to make words. An egg carton could be used instead of a shoe box and envelopes.

Catch a Rhyme: A game of catch can make a great rhyming word exercise. The child who catches the ball must say a word that rhymes with the one given. A variation of this is to use initial sounds.

Shapes and Sounds: Shapes are cut out of tagboard (or construction paper) and decorated to represent unit activities or holidays (Easter egg, Christmas package, pumpkin, etc.) A word ending is written on each shape. Two slits should be cut so that a strip of paper containing initial consonants may be pulled through. The child can make a new word by substituting different initial consonants.

Family House: A house is made from stiff paper or construction paper. Cut several windows out and glue a strip to form a pocket for the "family" name such as *ell* or *ame* (a word family previously studied). Give the child several small cards each with a consonant sound on them. The cards should fit in the windows of the house. Call the "children" (that is, known words that can be made by putting a consonant in the windows to make a word with the word family) to eat and see who comes to the table. A variation of this is to make a school house and call the roll to see which "children" (known words) are present. Another variation is to use a tree and branches for the word family and words.

Train Story: A picture is selected from a newspaper or magazine. The first child tells or writes the first sentence, or the "engine," of a story about the picture. The picture continues from child to child in this way with each one adding a "car" to the "train" until all the children have a turn.

Using the Newspaper: Use these activities with beginning readers:

1. Give each child a page from the newspaper. Have the children pretend to read "like Daddy." This is a good exercise in left-to-right practice.

2. Have the class select a picture from the newspaper. The teacher pastes the picture on posterboard. Then the children make up a story to go with the picture. This is then printed under the picture. The posterboard should be placed conveniently in the room so that the children can refer to it during the day.

3. Let each child pick out his own picture from the newspaper. Then he makes up his own story. This is written under the picture by the teacher or the child.

4. Give each child a sheet of newspaper. Have the children look for the "word of the day." The word is to be circled with a brightly colored crayon.

5. Comic sections from the Sunday newspaper can be used to make sequence cards. As the child progresses, he can read the story content. The comic sections should be glued on cardboard and laminated to last through classroom handling.

For advanced readers newspapers can be used in every subject. This is a good way to keep learning up-to-date and the child interested.

1. Collect words with different connotations (i.e., happy words, sad words, etc.). Cut them out and paste them on construction paper.

2. Frequently let the students read articles to the class. These may be from any section: sports, entertainment, front page, etc.

The uses of the newspaper are so myriad that they are only limited by the teacher's imagination.

In the Dark: Prepare a series of large cards with letters or numbers. The child traces over the pattern, using a small flashlight in a darkened room. This works well as a class project. Write large letters on the chalkboard; then, let each child have a turn at the board.

Junior Sand Pile: Fill shallow trays (pie pans or cake tins work nicely) with damp sand, salt, or damp clay. The child draws the required letters or shapes with his finger or stick.

CHAPTER 4

Science

Penny Paper Weights: Collect the following materials: New pennies, plaster-of-paris, masking tape, scissors, and an egg carton.

Nest, follow this procedure: Cut the bottom of the egg carton into 12 separate egg holders. Some of the holders will have open areas on the side, so tape should be placed across the open part. This will form a cup which will hold the plaster. Now, place a small piece of rolled tape in the bottom of the cup. This will hold the penny in place and keep the plaster from running under the penny. After the tape is in place, turn a penny face down in the bottom of the cup on the tape. Be sure to press down firmly so the penny will be secure. Now mix the plaster-of-paris, as directed on the package, and pour it into the cup. Fill it as full as desired, preferably to the top, and use a stick to gently pat so all the air bubbles will be forced out. It takes about five minutes to dry. Now, tear away the cup, and the penny paper weight is finished. If desired, sandpaper may be used to make it smoother, and the paper weights can, also, be painted. About twelve paper weights can be made from one pound of plaster-of-paris.

Play Clay: First, gather these materials: corn starch box, 2 cups baking soda, 1 cup corn starch, 1½ cup cold water, and food color if desired.

Mix corn starch and baking soda in a saucepan until thoroughly blended. Mix in water, adding a few drops of food coloring if desired. Cook over medium heat for about 4 minutes, stirring constantly until the mixture thickens to a moist mashed-potato consistency. Cover with damp cloth to cool. Knead as you would dough. Clay holds up well and does not crumble.

Dough may be rolled or molded. If rolled, it can be cut into any shape with cookie cutters. Let dry thoroughly overnight. Thick pieces may take longer to dry. Paint with tempera or water colors. Spray with clear shellac, clear plastic, or clear nail polish.

Jewelry, Christmas tree ornaments, etc. can be made.

Sweet Potato Plant: Place a sweet potato, sprouted end up, in a glass or jar of water. Water should be changed frequently; or put some charcoal in the bottom of the jar to help prevent decay. To start the plant, place in indirect light and a warm place. When it sprouts and makes shoots that are ready to climb, put it in a sunny window. If you want it to climb, place wires or sticks in or around the jar. If you want to make a pot plant, pinch shoots back to make it bushy. It takes two or three weeks for it to start.

Carrot Plant or Hanging Basket: Cut a carrot in half—press firmly into sand or peat moss. Leave about half of the carrot above the surface. If leaves have already sprouted on top of the carrot, trim and leave about half an inch. If you wish a hanging basket, cut the tip of the carrot off about two inches from the tip. Place three small holes through the carrot just above where you cut it off. Hollow out the center of the carrot. Do not get too close to the edges. Insert a piece of wire or string through the nail holes and bring them together at the top. Fill the hollow carrot with water and hang in the sun. It may be hung on a nail, a cup hook, or a clothes hanger.

Beet Plant: This may be treated like the carrot plant.

Miniature Garden or Park: Use pie tins or empty frozen-dinner aluminum "plates" as containers. Children may use any appropriate small articles to build their scenes: shells, dried moss, sand, popsicle sticks, twigs, etc.

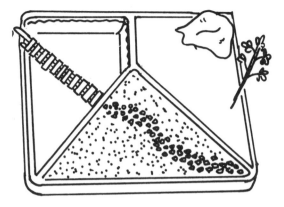

Did You Know? Green plants will not make the food required for growth without light? Try growing a green plant in the dark. If there is only a little light, the plant will try to grow toward it.

Garden: Grow a miniature garden on a sponge. Collect the following materials: Approximately one-inch sponge (cut into any shape), a bowl, water, and grass or bird seed.

    Then, saturate the sponge. Place seed in holes in the sponge. Set the bowl in a warm, dark area until the seeds sprout, then put it in a lighted area. Water when excess water in dish is gone. Seeds will sprout in several days. (Plants can be grown without soil. Kids love it.)

Celery Coloring: Show how water travels through the stem of plants. First, collect these materials: a drinking glass, a celery stalk with leaves, red ink, and water.

    Add red ink to one-half glass of water. Place the celery stalk in the glass, cut side down. Let stand overnight or several hours.

    The leaves should become red or veined in red. Cut the stem crosswise in several places. Note the results. (The stems carry water to the leaves through small tubes or pipes. This enables the plant to make its own food with the help of sunshine and other materials.)

Here are two more activities:

1. Split the celery stalk and put each end in separate jars or glasses, each with a different colored ink.

2. White flowers may be colored in this manner.

Seeds: Seeds may be sprouted by placing between two pieces of glass held together by a rubber band. Stand the pieces of glass upright in a pan of water and observe results daily.

Seeds also may be sprouted by placing seeds between two moist pieces of paper towel.

Beans soaked overnight can be opened up so the children can see the new plant growth that is beginning.

Storage Battery: Make a simple battery. Gather these materials: 1 juicy lemon, 1 thin strip zinc, and 1 thin strip lead. (A carbon rod and piece of the zinc cover of a dry cell battery, both well sanded, may be substituted for the zinc and lead strips. A dead battery may be used.) Cut two slits in the lemon as shown, put the strip of zinc in one slit, and put the strip of lead or the cleaned carbon rod in the other slit. Touch your tongue across the two metal strips. You should feel a slight tingle in your tongue.

You have created electrical energy from chemical energy.

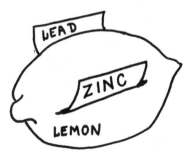

Paper Bag See-Saw: What happens when air is heated? Gather these materials: 3 pieces of string, 1 yardstick, 2 small paper bags, 1 candle or hot plate, and matches.

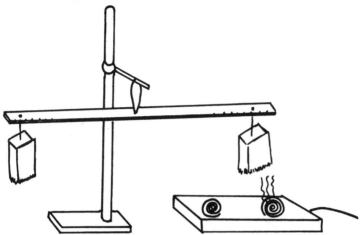

Drill holes, two inches from each end of the yardstick, and one in the center of the yardstick. Attach paper bags to each end of the yardstick as shown in the diagram. Suspend the yardstick in the middle so it will swing freely. Try to get it balanced. Light the candle and hold it under one bag and then the other (not too close). The warm air rises and causes the bag to rise; cool air sinks.

This principle can be used to illustrate how clouds are formed. This is good to use to show how your school room may be cooler on the floor than it is at the top of the room. A spiral can be cut out of construction paper and suspended by the center on a pencil point. Put a candle under it and it will turn.

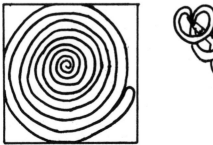

41

Jet Boat: Make a boat that is jet propelled. Collect these materials: A flat three-inch by five-inch board (or a ready-made boat from the store), a balloon, the glass part of a medicine dropper, and a rubber band or some sort of clip.

Make a flat board shaped like a boat. Attach a balloon (blown up) to the board with a clip or rubber band as shown in the diagram. Place the boat in a tub of water or place several *round* pencils under it on the floor. Release the air in the balloon and observe what happens.

The boat will move in the direction opposite the direction the air is coming out of the balloon. (For every action there is an equal and opposite reaction.)

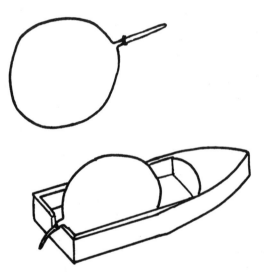

Magic Boat: Make a boat move with a magnet. Use these materials: A flat piece of two-inch by three and a half-inch cork, several tin tacks, a stick or ruler, a horseshoe magnet, string, and a pan of water on blocks—just higher than the magnet.

sail. Attach the magnet to stick as shown in diagram. Place sail boat (with tin tacks pushed into the underside) in the pan of water. The pan must be on blocks high enough for the magnet to be slipped under the pan of water and then move the magnet around under the pan. Tin tacks become magnetized and the boat moves around as you move the magnet.

Salt Dough: To make salt dough, use these materials: 1 cup salt, 2 cups unsifted flour, 1 tablespoon powdered alum (optional), and approximately 1 cup water.

Mix together salt, flour, and alum. Add water a little at a time until the mixture resembles pie dough. Alum makes it more pliable and easier to work with.

This dough can be used to make maps or models of any kind. It has a tendency to crumble when it hardens or gets old. Do not handle too much. The body heat of the hands makes it soft and sticky.

Simple Pulley: Gather these materials: 2 large thread spools, 2 pieces of easily bent wire (about a foot long) or two coat hangers, 3 cup hooks, a weight, and about 4 feet of string or cord.

Put wire through spool and bend. Put one hook into the top of a frame. Attach wire and hook to second spool. Attach one end of string to the hook at the top of the frame, thread it down and around second spool then back up over the top of the first spool, leaving one end free to pull. Attach a weight to the bottom hook and pull down on the free string.

By using a pulley system, two weights may be lifted more easily. You do exactly the same amount of work, but with more ease.

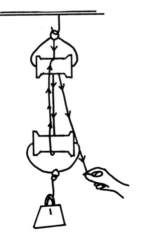

Rainbow of Colors: How can you make a rainbow without a prism? Gather these materials: a pan of water (shallow), a mirror, and a light source such as sunlight or the light beam from a projection lamp.

Place a mirror at an angle inside the water filled pan. Place the pan in the path of a strong source of light so that the rays strike the mirror in the water. A rainbow should reflect on the wall or a sheet of white paper.

Light can be broken down into a rainbow of colors: red, orange, yellow, green, blue, and violet.

The principle involved shows how a rainbow of colors is formed in the sky when the sun's rays reflect off of the water droplets, why a diamond sparkles, and how a prism breaks down light. It also helps to show how light rays are refracted or bent.

Crystal Rock Garden: Use these materials: 4 tablespoons bluing, 4 tablespoons salt, 2 tablespoons household ammonia, merthiolate, or food coloring, 4 tablespoons hot water, and a sponge, paper towel, or charcoal briquet.

Mix all ingredients and pour over either sponge, charcoal briquets, or crumbled paper towel. Merthiolate or food color may be mixed into the mixture; or it may be sprinkled on the top of the mixture; or if desired, the mixture may be left white. Different colors may be added as the crystals begin to grow.

Electric Quiz Game: You can construct a quiz board using switches and wire, or you can purchase a board already constructed. Completion of the proper circuit will give the correct answer.

Use these materials; a commercial bulb, any desired number of switches, insulated wire, plug, and a board to mount the switches on.

Place questions beside one set of switches and a set of answers by the second set of switches. Be sure to scramble them up. The child reads the questions and tries to come up with the correct answer. When he is ready to try the board to see if he is right, he pushes down on the switch with the question with one finger and pushes down on the switch which he thinks has the right answer with the other hand. If his choice of answers is correct, the bulb will light up. This gives instant response, which children love. Correct answer—bulb lights up; incorrect answer—no light.

An electric current must be completed before electricity will flow through a circuit. By varying the questions and cross connections, this can be used as a teaching device in many subjects.

A commercial hobby shop will probably have a quiz game board. If they do not, ask them to make you up one if you can't do it yourself. Some of the better equipped toy stores carry quiz game boards of all kinds. They might be adapted to your needs.

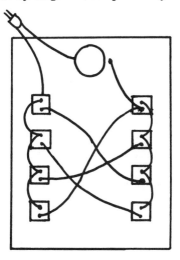

Magnetism: Show children that magnets have two different poles: a "north" pole and a "south" pole.

Use these materials: 2 bar magnets, a sheet of white paper, and iron filings.

First, place opposite ends of the bar magnet about one inch apart. Place the sheet of paper on top of them and sprinkle lightly with iron filings. (You may have to tap the iron filings lightly to make the pattern clear.) Filings will outline the magnetic field showing that unlike poles attract each other. Second, perform the experiment again, except placing like ends of magnets together. Filings will outline the magnetic field showing that like poles repel each other. This shows that bar magnets have polarity (two different poles).

Bar magnets and horseshoe magnets can be used to pick up many different metal objects. A horseshoe magnet will show polarity also.

Activities: Test several items: screw, pennies, eraser, pins, wood, chalk, paper, and scissors. Make two lists: "Magnets Attract" and "Magnets Do Not Attract." Try several of the items listed above, or others, and put them in the column where they fit best.

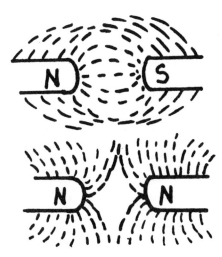

CHAPTER 5

Social Studies

Class Directory: A very good get-acquainted idea is to start the first week of school by taking pictures of each student in the room.   (A Polaroid or similar instant-developing camera is recommended.)   The teacher needs a picture of herself also.   Address, telephone number, birthday, and parents' name are entered on sheets of paper.   Let the children arrange the sheets in alphabetical order.   Attach pictures to correct papers.   Put these into a folder or a notebook.   This directory comes in handy for sending birthday cards, holiday cards, making home visits, and numerous other things.

Field Trip: You can take a field trip to "find" each child's home.   This helps them to locate different areas in the community and is also a good chance for each child to be "special."   Include the teacher's house—possibly with some refreshments.

Community Map: Build your immediate community in your schoolroom by using masking tape on the floor for streets and sidewalks and large cardboard boxes for buildings.   The boxes can be painted to resemble the school's closest shopping center.   Purposes of stores can be discussed as well as traffic signals, safety signs, and rules (toy bicycles and model automobiles could be used).

Newspaper Private Eye: (For older students.) Atypical children are often unaware of the world around them because of their inability to read a newspaper. One simple way to increase their awareness as well as their vocabulary is to play "Newspaper Private Eye." Hang front pages from newspapers or such papers as "Know Your World" (one for each student) on the walls around the class at eye level. Tell the class that they are detectives and must search for a "clue." Give each student an index card on which a word taken from one of the newspaper headlines is printed. Have them walk around the room until the correct page is found. The students stand in front of their pages until their "clues" are checked. After "clues" are checked, the cards may be shuffled and given out again, Adaptations are limitless; if you are doing a unit on shopping, the pages containing the supermarket ads can be used for the game. If you are studying a unit on leisure time, use the sports pages and theatre ads. This game is fun and easy to plan; the materials are cheap and reusable. The game is also excellent as a remedial method for figure-ground reversal problems.

Community Key People: Each of the people in the following list plays an important role in the community. Using puppets made in arts and crafts let students play the role of each in regard to duties, services, responsibilities, needs, and importance in the community. Play "Charades" by having some members of the class act out the different occupations and let the others "guess who."

1. mayor
2. policeman
3. fireman
4. mailman
5. doctor
6. dentist
7. nurse

Map Reading: Social studies may be introduced by map reading. The pupils will want to learn their way around the school, home, and community. On the floor, place two large sheets of paper which have been fastened together. These sheets of paper should be four or five yards long so the pupils can walk on them. Highways and roads are designated and intersections with stop signs are added. Different towns within a thirty-mile radius are placed on the map.

Month of the Year: A large (preferably 20-foot) bulletin board is prepared by the teacher. The children add art work symbolizing the month. Ribbons lead from dates to the appropriate areas.

Indian Sign Language: When studying the early days of our country, the children will enjoy learning about Indian tribes and their cultures. One activity that can be introduced is learning Indian sign language. The teacher may either let the children make up their own sign language, or she may find it helpful to use references to learn sign language used by the Indians. One book is *Indian Sign Language* by William Tomkins. The Boy Scout Handbook also carries 40 or 50 communication signs. After the children have learned several of the signs, allow them a certain period during the day in which they must communicate only with the hands.

Picture Lotto: Use large picture cards made from tagboard, and pictures of birds, animals, community helpers, etc. cut from magazines. The different names are written under the picture. As the name of the item is called, it is covered. The first child covering all the items correctly wins.

Tree Game: To be a tree detective, the students should be able to use clues to find out names of trees. The trees used should be common in the area. A chart should be constructed (pictures can be obtained from the State Wildlife and Parks Department). Take the chart along with students on a field trip. The students are to name the tree from its leaf, needle, flower, or bud.

CHAPTER 6

Arts

Music

Sticks Game: Give each child two rhythm sticks. Use a record with a strong rhythmic beat, preferably one without singing. Have the students follow the teacher in various rhythmic activities, such as touching sticks, touching various parts of the body, touching the floor, touching a chair, etc.

Colors Game: Give each child two strips of crepe paper, each a different color. Use a record with a strong rhythmic beat, preferably one without singing. Then have the students follow the teacher's verbal directions, such as, "Raise the red paper." "Put the green paper behind your back." When the group becomes accustomed to this routine, give two directions at the same time, such as, "Put the green paper on your head, and the red paper on your shoulder." As a variation, give each child two flags of the same color to follow spatial directions, such as, "up," "down," "right," etc.

Dramatization: Most songs and instrumental music can be dramatized. This brings the words or the music of the song directly into the life of the child. Simple costumes can be made by the teacher or child from old sheets, cardboard boxes, paper sacks, or old clothes. The characters can be brought into the classroom.

Finger Painting to Music: Finger painting to various types of music can bring physical and emotional enjoyment to a child. The music may be soft and soothing at one time and strong and pulsating at another time. Encourage creativity.

Flannel Board Characters with Song: Use flannel figures to teach sequence, vocabulary, and visual attention. Put the figure on the board when it is time for it in the song. This technique is good for songs such as "Little White Duck," and "There Was An Old Woman Who Swallowed A Fly." Here are some variations:

1. Flash cards can be used for this same purpose. Change gradually from pictures to words to help chldren in reading.
2. A sequence game can be played wherein the teacher puts the figures out of sequence, and a child has to identify what is wrong.
3. Many children enjoy playing the figures on the flannel board themselves as the song progresses.
4. Each child could have a different character to
   · put on the flannel board when it is his turn in the sequence.

Small characters can be made out of tagboard and a small piece of magnetic tape put on the back for use on a magnetic board.

Rhythms: The teacher claps a rhythm, and the student imitates it. As the students progress in this, the teacher can add and mix snapping, tapping, and patting knees in a rhythmic pattern. This activity can be performed with or without music.

Puppets: Use puppets to represent characters in songs, such as commercially available Sesame Street or Charlie Brown puppets, and handmade sock, paper plate, paper sack, or glove puppets.

Music Bingo: Use a heavy piece of cardboard divided into squares, each square having a picture in it representing a song. Make one divided cardboard sheet for each child. The children use tokens or buttons to cover the picture representing the song being played. More advanced readers can just use the words in place of the pictures.

Musical Bean Bag: While a song is playing, the children pass a bean bag around the circle. When the song is stopped, each child must name the letter which he holds. Each can say a word or name beginning with that sound. Other items which can be used: pictures of food, clothing, etc.

Arts and Crafts

Glue Picture: The child can make a simple design with glue on tagboard. After the glue has dried sufficiently, he can paint the entire piece of tagboard with watercolors. The paint will not adhere to the dried glue (which is now clear). The glue design or picture will stand out.

Charcoal Drawing: Pieces of charcoal can be used to make a design or picture on newspaper. Tagboard figures or templates can be traced with charcoal.

Burlap Pictures: Using burlap, which can often be obtained from feed stores, and large needles and yarn, the children can sew at random or on a design. Table mats, belts, small purses, etc. can be made.

Eggshell Pictures: Use crushed eggshells to make a picture. Use construction paper for background. Eggshells. may be dyed with food coloring.

Spring Flower: Cut a three inch square of construction paper and fold in half:

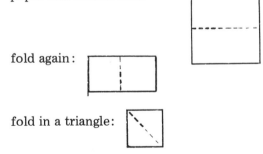

fold again:

fold in a triangle:

with the folded edges down, cut a semicircle:

57

Unfold. Make two and glue together overlapping the petals. Wad a piece of tissue paper up for the center. Glue on a pipecleaner stem.

Picture Print: Use string, styrofoam packaging, wadded foil, or still paper to dip into tempera paint. Holding one of these with a clothespin or with fingers, press it onto the paper or move it lightly across the paper to make a "print." Other items which acan be used: pencil, tongue depressors, paper clips, erasers, and plastic forks.

Handprints: (This can be done after finger painting.) Each child makes his handprint on a sheet of drawing paper. A bulletin board can be made with handprints. The teacher draws and paints the trunk of a tree. Each child comes up and puts his green handprint above the trunk to make leaves.

Spaghetti Mobile: Cook one package of long spaghetti and cool. Dip spaghetti in a mixture of powdered tempera, glue, and a small amount of water. Drop spaghetti on a piece of tin foil in connected abstract or representational designs. Let dry in a dry place for three days. Peel off the foil. Hang from string.

A Fall Tree: Draw a big tree outline on paper. Cover the top with glue and shake confetti over it. Make confetti from fall colors using light-weight paper. Cover the trunk of the tree with tiny rocks using glue.

Pressed Nature Picture: Collect flowers, leaves, ferns, etc. Dry them by pressing them between sheets of newspaper weighted with heavy objects. Let them dry one week. Cover a piece of cardboard with material and tape in place. Arrange the dry, pressed flowers, etc. into a design and glue them in place. Frame the finished picture.

Tissue Puffs: Each child has an outline of a picture and several one-inch squares of colored tissue paper. Pick up one square of the colored tissue paper. Put it on the unsharpened end of a pencil. Fold and squeeze the paper around the pencil. The paper will stay shaped like a little cup around the pencil. Hold the paper around the pencil and dip the end in paste. Set the pasted end on the picture, and lift up the pencil. Shape a second piece and paste it beside the first one. Fill in the entire picture.

Blowing Pictures: The child chooses a piece of construction paper and a color. The teacher places a small amount of the food coloring on the child's paper. The child blows at the coloring through a straw. Other colors may be used for blending. Let the finished product dry. Tempera paint can be used instead of food coloring.

Foot Pictures: Trace around a child's foot. Let him draw a picture around his traced foot or including it. Let him color it.

Finger Paint Print: Squeeze starch on a formica table top. Sprinkle tempera on the starch; several colors may be blended. Finger paint the entire table top, using parts of the hand and arm. Press a piece of finger-paint paper down on top of the painting and peel it off. Clean the table top with sponges. Let the prints dry.

Resist: Color a picture with crayons. Cover the entire surface of the paper with watercolor paint. The paint will be absorbed by the uncolored paper and resisted by the wax crayons.

Chalk Art: Here are several activities the children will enjoy:

1. Make chalk pictures on construction paper. Light chalk on dark paper will aid the child in interpreting subjects which are light in value, such as snow. Chalk on gray paper will allow contrasts in both light and dark chalk. Chalk on colored paper will allow contrasts depending on the colors used. Spray with a fixative (hair spray works very well) and allow to dry.

2. Make chalk pictures on coarse sandpaper. The sandpaper can be dry or wet. Spray with a fixative or laminate when finished.

3. Dampen paper with a damp sponge. Draw over the damp paper with chalk. Note: Chalk sticks, soaked for ten minutes in a strong solution of sugar water and allowed to dry before use, reduce the tendency to smear.

Potato Printing: To prepare the potatoes, choose firm potatoes. Cut crosswise or lengthwise so edges are straight and will rest flat on the surface to be printed. Trim the top part slightly to form a handle so that a child can grasp the potato easily.

To make the design, cut out a paper design and with a pencil, trace around the design on the cut surface of the potato. Using a sharp paring knife, cut along pencil lines one quarter inch deep. Carefully slice in from the outer edge of potato, cutting around design and removing excess potato to raise the design.

To make the paint pad, choose appropriate colors. The paint should be fairly thick. Pour a small amount of each color into individual bowls containing a folded cloth or paper towel. Let the potato printer stand on paint pad long enough to absorb paint.

Store the potato printer in a plastic bag in the refrigerator.

Pine Cone Bird Feeder: Each child is given a pine cone. Peanut butter can be pressed into the cracks of the pine cone, or the pine cone can be rolled in a bowl of peanut butter. Bird seed is then sprinkled all over the pine cone, and it will stick to the peanut butter. A piece of yarn or string is tied to the stem or to one of the "petals." It can be hung from low tree branches or tied to a fence.

Plastic Bottle Bird Feeder: Cut holes in the sides of a large plastic bottle and hang string or yarn from it. Bird seed or bits of table food can be placed in the bottom. Feeders have to be large and sturdy enough for the birds to perch comfortably. Punch drainage holes in the bottom of your feeders.

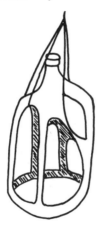

Pillow Picture: The teacher starches an old pillow case very stiff. (This could be done in class.) Then she, or the child, cuts the pillow case to the desired shape. It can be colored with crayon.

Happiness Rock: Ask each child to bring to school a rock that he or she likes because of its texture, shape, or color. Put these rocks on a table along with a collection of magazines, scissors, white glue, and paste dabbers. Have available shellac, paint brushes, and wax paper. Each child may find pictures in a magazine of his favorite color or pictures of things that make him think of happiness. He glues the pictures on his rock, allows it to dry, and then puts shellac over it.

Sheets of Fun: Use an old sheet for children to color and make designs on. Crayons can be used. This could become a mural or a room divider. At Thanksgiving the "Indian-designed" sheet can be wrapped around four bamboo sticks fastened at the top to make a tepee.

Drawing with Yarn: Dip eight to ten inch lengths of yarn in starch. Wind and drop the yarn on a piece of cardboard. Let dry. When dry, color each space; the hardened yarn serves to limit spaces.

Bird House: Cover a one-quart milk carton with brown paper (perhaps from a paper bag). Cut a two-inch hole in the front with a half-inch hole right below it going out the back. Cover the brown paper with very small sticks which have been sliced down the middle. These can be glued into the half-inch hole in front for a perch.

CHAPTER 7

Physical Activities

The room shown in the diagram below contains a great number of possibilities for sequenced motor activities. If the classroom teacher does not have this much room available, she should choose as many and as varied activities as possible within the limits of space.

The constant shifting of balance and movement increases the child's *body schema* and *body image*. The verbalization of these activities increases the child's *body concept*.

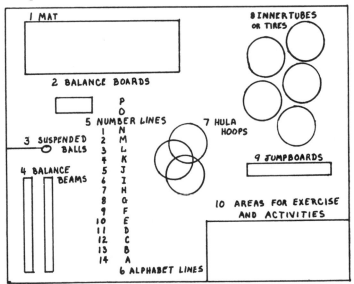

Mat Activities

These activities are all excellent for developing gross-motor coordination as well as concepts of laterality and directionality. Although the classroom teacher may not have access to regular gymnastic mats, things such as throw rugs, towels, or blankets work just as well.

Children will enjoy all the rolls. Examples of these are the log rolls, forward and backward rolls. Besides the regular tumbling-type activities, boys may enjoy combatives.

Examples of the combative activities are:

Push-Over:

1. The two opponents assume standard "up" wrestling position, with the exception that both opponents are standing on their knees.
2. On the "start" signal, competitors attempt to push one another over without moving knees. The winner is the last competitor to move his knees.

Nimble Jack:

1. The two competitors are shoeless.
2. Competitors assume the standard "up" wrestling position.
3. On the "start" signal, opponents attempt to step on each other's feet, while protecting their own feet.
4. Game continues until "stop" signal is given.

Chicken Fight:

1. The two or more opponents assume the squatting position: arms to inside of knees and hands grasp outside of ankle.
2. On the "start" signal, opponents, by bumping into each other, attempt to push all other opponents over and remain in the game position.
3. The last remaining in the correct position is the winner.

Knuckle Spread:

1. One of the two competitors makes a fist with

each hand. He then puts the first and second sets of knuckles of each hand together (thumbs toward body). The opponent stands facing the competitor and grabs the arms (just above the wrists).

2. On the "start" signal, the opponent attempts to pull the two fists apart (not jerk).

3. Variation: Finger spread instead of putting knuckles together, one opponent can put his two first fingers together.

Back to Back:

1. Opponents stand back to back, step forward one step, step to right one step (or left), raise left (or right) hands, depending on direction of step, and hook first fingers.

2. On the "start" signal, opponents, without moving feet, attempt to pull (not jerk) opponent off balance.

3. The winner is the competitor who last moves a foot or feet.

Leg Wrestle:

1. Opponents lie supine next to each other with heads in opposite directions, elbows hooked.

2. On "start" signal, teacher says "one" and "two" and opponents raise the inside leg straight up, and put it back down. On the count of "three" opponents raise inside leg and hook opponent's raised leg. Opponents attempt to push each other over, using only one leg.

Arm Wrestle:

1. Opponents lie prone with heads facing each other. With the right hand (or left), grasp opponent's same hand. Keep elbows on the floor and upper arms perpendicular to the floor.

2. On the "start" signal opponents attempt to push each other's hand to the floor.

3. The match can last until a winner is declared (or a time limit may be set).

Dragon's Mouth:

1. All students stand around outside edge of a mat.
2. On a given signal, students push each other onto the mat.
3. The game continues until all but one participant is on the mat.

Island Flight:

1. Use a mat arrangement—four tumbling mats arranged in a square, leaving an open area in middle.
2. All students stand in the open area. On a given signal all students push each other onto the mats.
3. The game continues until only one participant remains in the open area.

Rid'em:

1. The "down" man is on hands and knees. The "up" man places his chest on the "down" man's back. The "up" man balances with his feet, and cannot use his hands.
2. On the "start" signal, the "down" man begins crawling in any direction, attempting to crawl out from under the "up" man.

Scalp'em:

1. Opponents assume standard "up" wrestling position. Opponents stand with feet wider than shoulder width, right hand placed behind the opponent's neck, and left hand grasping the opponent's right wrist.
2. On the "start" signal, competitors attempt to pull the opponent's right hand off his own neck, while keeping one's own right hand on the opponent's neck.

Slap Opposite Knee:

1. Opponents assume the standard "up" wrestling position, with the exception that the left arm and hand are free.

2. On the "start" signal, competitors attempt to slap the inside of the opponent's left knee, while protecting one's own left knee.

Balance Beam Activities: (The child is to keep his eyes on a target.)

1. Walk forward across the board.
2. Walk forward and carry a weight in hand.
3. Walk forward and carry a weight, shifting the weight from hand to hand.
4. Walk backward across the board.
5. Walk forward and backward, balancing an eraser on one's head.
6. Walk forward and backward and bounce a ball.
7. Walk sideways across the board and lead with the right foot, then the left.
8. Walk across the board with arms extended to the sides, then to the front, back, both to one side, then both to the other.
9. Walk forward and pick up an eraser from the middle of the beam.
10. Walk to the center of the board and step over a wand held 12 inches above the beam.
11. Walk to the center of the board, catch a bean bag, and pitch it back to the teacher.
12. Hop on right or left foot the length of beam.
13. Walk to the center of the board, kneel on one knee, and straighten the other leg forward until heel is on beam and knee is straight.
14. Place hands on hips and squat and walk under the wand at various heights above the beam.
15. Walk to the center of the beam, close eyes, and see how long balance can be maintained.

Lines on Floor:

1. Place cut-outs of footprints on the floor and have the child walk in exact steps. Have him cross over, and use alternate feet.
2. Walk a straight line placed on floor and perform stunts done on balance beam.

3. Walk a zig-zag line placed on floor with masking tape.

4. Walk to certain numbers placed on a line on the floor. Stop at certain numbers and return.

5. Walk the alphabet line and recognize certain letters. Try to encourage them to verbalize.

6. Play games similar to hopscotch.

Animal Walks:

1. "Monkey Roll"—Three at a time perform on a mat a series of figure-eights in which they roll under and jump over at the same time.

2. "Wheelbarrow"—The child walks on his hands while a partner holds his feet suspended in the air.

3. "Bear Walk"—Walk on all fours.

4. "Crab Walk"—Walk on all fours in reverse position.

5. "Rabbit Walk"—Walk on all fours but move both hands simultaneously and feet alternately moved simultaneously.

6. "Dead Elephant Walk"—Place weight on hands and walk dragging legs.

Zoo: The children form a circle. Each child will take a turn in the center of the circle and perform one of the animal walks. The observing children attempt to guess which animal he is portraying.

Hoop Activities:

1. Place a hoop on the floor and step in, out, and around the hoop.

2. Find as many different ways as you can to go around the hoop.

3. Place different parts of the body inside the hoop.

4. Throw bean bags into the hoop.

5. Roll the hoop.

6. Jump with the hoop.

7. Spin the hoop.

8. Move through a hoop that is moving.

9. With one person holding the hoop, have a partner climb through in as many ways as possible.
10. Turn circles with a hoop on one's arm, leg, waist, or neck.
11. Throw the hoop into the air and catch it.
12. Play catch with a partner.
13. Make obstacles with hoops on chairs.
14. Suspend a hoop from the ceiling and throw different kinds of balls through the hoop.

Tire Activities: Old tires can be used either indoors or out, and are inexpensive and easy to obtain. A large variety of activities can be performed with the tires. These activities are:

1. Walk around the rim of the tire.
2. Run or walk backwards around the tires.
3. Run around the tires weaving various patterns.
4. Use any locomotor activity to get around the tires.
5. Think of different ways to get around tires.
6. Step in and out of the tires.
7. Stand and jump into a tire.
8. Use various rhythm patterns to jump in and out of the tires.
9. Place a scarf on the rim of the tire and have the student jump to face the scarf; then place the scarf at a different position and have the child jump again.
10. Stand in a tire and jump upward.
11. Jump out of the tire from a crouch position.
12. Hop, bunny-jump, or frog-jump from tire to tire.
13. Place hands on the tire and walk around the tire with hands and feet.
14. Roll the tire to anther person.
15. Toss bean bags into the tires.
16. Place a weight inside the tire and roll it.
17. Stack several tires, one on top of another and

have the children climb in and out of the tires.

18. Use tires in an obstacle course.

Classroom Ball Activities

A Yarn Ball: To make this ball, you will need one skein of yarn, a piece of cardboard five inches by ten inches and some light strong cord for binding. Wrap yarn 20 to 25 times around cardboard. Slide yarn off the cardboard and tie in middle with cord. Continue until all cord is used. Take two loops and tie together at centers, using several turns of the cord, as illustrated. Next, tie bundles together by pairs. Then form a ball by tying the paired bundles together until all are used.

A Paper Ball: This is another type of ball that will help teach the concepts of *ball* and *roundness*. Give each child a large piece of paper; a sheet or two of newspaper will do nicely. Have children "make a ball" by crumpling the paper into a ball shape. Use masking tape to hold the ball in this shape. By using something the children have made, motivation to participate will be very high.

A Nerf or Fleece Ball: These are very soft balls which are good for classroom activities. To make a ball on a string, tie a piece of cord into the center of the yarn ball; or, using a large needle, thread a heavy string through the paper or the Nerf ball. Tennis balls make excellent balls on a string.

Assorted Activities:

1. Have the children roll the balls to each other in both sitting and standing positions. Have them roll the balls between their partner's legs with their partner's back to them. The partner tries to catch the ball as it rolls between his legs.

2. Have children kick the balls to partners or have a partner roll a ball to a child for this child to kick back to the partner.

3. Try throwing the balls while standing still

and while walking slowly in pairs across the room.

4. Throw balls at targets drawn with chalk on the board or into baskets or ball barrels.

5. Play "Prickly Pear" using one or two balls passed quickly around a seated circle. Use a kitchen timer bell or some other signal to indicate time to stop passing the balls. Those caught with the balls must pay a penalty (leave the circle, sing a song, sit in the middle, recite the ABC's).

6. Have children paint some three pound coffee cans with bright colors or decorate the cans with pieces of paper glued on. Have the children work in pairs, using the cans as scoops. Use the can to toss the ball to a partner who tries to catch it in his can. Scoops could also be made from plastic bleach bottles or similar items.

7. Play "Dog and Cat" in a seated circle. Start one colored ball passing quickly in the circle. After a few passes, start a different colored ball. The first ball is the Cat, the second, the Dog. Tell the children to try and have the Dog catch the Cat, but to try and not let the Cat get caught.

8. Try throwing balls through rolling hoops of different sizes.

9. Have the children work in pairs using balls on a string. Have one child lie on the floor with the other child standing above the head of the first, holding the ball on a string a few inches above the face of the first child. Have the standing child swing the ball slowly back and forth over the face of the first. The lying child must track the ball with his eyes and one finger.

10. Have each child hold a ball on a string in one hand, arm extended, ball hanging about waist high. Using the dominant hand as a racket, have the child hit the ball from the

bottom, the top, and the side. Tell them to always watch the ball for practice in visual tracking.

Suspended Ball Activities:

1. Alternate hitting the ball back and forth with right and left hands.
2. Hit the ball with one's head. (Clasp hands behind back.)
3. Hit the ball with alternate hands on command. Be sure to have the children follow the ball with their eyes as it swings in space.
4. Tap the ball with a bat and count number of consecutive taps.

Barrels In The Classroom

Here are three things you can make using large cardboard industrial barrels like those that soap or chemicals come in.

Target Barrels: Cut a hole, large enough for a playground ball to pass through, at the bottom of a barrel. Place an oval piece of plywood in the bottom and slope it toward the opening to provide a ball return. Paint the barrel colorfully to transform it into a grinning clown or other cartoon character. Use the barrel like a basketball hoop.

Rolling and Crawling Barrels: Cut the bottom out of the barrel. Paint the barrel with bright colors and designs. Use this barrel as a crawling tunnel or to roll over and over in. When set upon its end, this barrel can also be used as a target barrel without a ball return.

Wishing Well Barrels: Paint a barrel to resemble the bottom part of a wishing well. Attach a wooden frame to the top and sides of the barrel similar to that of a well. Fix a pulley in the center of the top crosspiece and suspend a bucket from a rope running through the pulley. Make different size weights from plaster or concrete poured into coffee cans. Have a child pull the rope to raise and lower the weights that have been placed in the bucket. For variation, have tasks or privileges written on cards that are placed in the bucket. The child goes to the well, pulls the rope, and reads a card. Then he must follow directions on the card. This activity is excellent for wheelchair-bound students.

Nerf Ball: This is an active game which can easily be played in the classroom or in a resource room by moving the chairs back. It is played like tennis, by hitting the sponge rubber ball back and forth over a line placed on the floor. Materials you will need: Nerf ball or ball made of sponge (should be soft and light, and could even be made of paper), two wire clothes hangers, electricians tape, and an old pair of panty hose. The clothes hangers should be shaped in form of tennis racket, and wire twisted together for handle. Tape the handle together. Slip old panty hose over wire and pull tight to form a racket and then wind excess around handle and tape.

Chinese Dishrag: Place Nerf ball or soft sponge ball between the heads of two children lying face down with their heads against the ball. Ask them to come to a standing position from the prone position without dropping the ball.

Four Square: This game is played with a soft rubber playground ball and court can easily be drawn off in the classroom with chalk or masking tape. A child guards each of the four squares; as the ball is bounced into a given court, the child tries to return it to another court. The game is played much like handball.

Challenge: This is a game to challenge the children's imagination. Ask them to lie on their stomachs, and hold both feet. Then tell them to come to a standing position without losing grip of their feet.

Geotwist: The geotwist may be easily made by placing several different colored geometric shapes on a 52" by 53" piece of vinyl cloth. Then, movement problems may be written on file cards. Examples of these movement problems are:

1. Place your head on the red circle.
2. Put one foot on the yellow square.
3. Place your left hand on the blue rectangle.

To play the game, shuffle the cards and allow the first player to draw a card. He must follow the directions on the card and then choose another card. He must follow the directions on this card without removing the preceding body part from the grid. He continues in this manner until he can no longer follow the directions. At this point the number of directions with which he was able to comply are added up and those are his points. The cards are returned to the deck and another player begins.

The geotwist may be used in a number of other ways. The child may be asked simply to jump from shape to shape or to hop on certain shapes. In this way he learns colors and shapes and gains skill in sequencing.

Percept-o-grid: The percept-o-grid is a large (36" by 99") piece of vinyl cloth on which squares are drawn. Numbers or letters are placed in the squares.

A number of activities are possible with the percept-o-grid. Children may toss bean bags at the grid, jump or hop into certain squares, jump or hop out words, or jump or hop out number problems.*

2	1	26	14	23	24	5	18	30
E	L	Z	K	D	A	J	I	
17	22	3	15	32	4	31	9	19
M	B	R	N	C	E	Y	S	N
27	7	34	16	6	11	35	10	24
H	G	T	R	Z	W	O	E	D
28	21	8	20	33	13	12	36	25
V	A	K	L	P	U	V	C	E

Bean Bag Activities: Bean bags are invaluable materials for motor activities in a classroom setting. The children may be given movement problems individually and with partners to solve with their bean bags. These might include:

    1. How high can you toss your bean bag into the air and catch it?

*For a variety of games, refer to *Active Learning: Games to Enhance Academic Abilities* by Bryant J. Cratty.

2. Can you toss your bean bag into the air and then clap your hands before you catch it?

3. Can you jump up and toss your bean bag into the air?

4. Can you balance your bean bag on your head and walk forward; backward; sideways?

5. Can you toss your bean bag to your partner? How many times without missing?

Many games may be invented with bean bags. Children may toss them into "goals" such as waste baskets or boxes. They may play a type of shuffle-board scooting the bean bag on the floor into a target. (Any kind of target-throwing is an excellent exercise in visual tracking.) Actually, almost any game that may be played with balls can be modified for bean bags.

Variation: Bean bags shaped as letters which are easily confused, such as *M* and *W*, *P* and *B*, *N* and *U*, and *D* and *B*, may be used to help children distinguish these letters. Examples (working with *M* and *W*):

1. Can you hold up a *W*?

2. (Place both bean bags on the floor.) Hop next to the *M*.

3. Put your left hand on the *W*.

Boxes: Cardboard boxes of various sizes large enough for a child to get inside may be placed throughout the room. The children are then given various movement problems to solve using the boxes. Examples of problems are:

1. Can you move quickly around your box without touching it?

2. Can you move over your box?

3. Can you get inside your box and fill up as much space as possible?

Also, games such as "Fruit Basket Turnover" and "Musical Chairs" may be played, the boxes being substituted for chairs.

Flash Cards: Flash cards for this activity are made by drawing stick figures on five- by eight-inch cards. The figures should have their arms and legs in different positions. As each card is shown to the children, they must position their own arms and legs in order to look like the figure.

Human Obstacle Course: The children are arranged in a single-file line. They are instructed that one of them is going to take a walk through the forest. The others are going to be obstacles that are found in a forest, such as trees, rocks, a river, a bridge, etc. Each child then decides which obstacle he will be and positions himself accordingly. The "walker" then moves around, over, under, or through all the obstacles on his way through the forest. The children will enjoy taking turns being the walker and thinking of different obstacles to be.

Obstacle Race: An obstacle course may be set up with practically any number of objects. Chairs, ropes, desks, boxes, etc. may be placed in a course for the children to walk over, under, around, and through. Obstacle courses are exciting for the children and are helpful in developing laterality, directionality, and gross-motor coordination.

Plastic Tube Activities: Activities with plastic tubes tend to enhance aspects of directionality, laterality, and kinesthetic awareness through nonverbal communication. As a form of movement education, the child may mirror the leader's movements, become the leader, or create his own individual movement patterns. The child finds success in any variation of this activity, since there is no failure and since he is allowed to release tension in a constructive manner. Other instructions:

1. Identify the color or length of the tube.
2. Tap tubes on the floor to create loud or soft sounds.
3. Bend and stretch with the tubes as exercises are performed.
4. Touch various parts of the body with tubes.
5. Blow tubes, when on the floor.
6. Balance tubes in hand or on the floor.

7. Throw and catch tubes.

8. Work with a partner and mirror movement.

9. Use tubes as an aid in balance activities on other equipment.

Rulers, pencils, and other objects may be used. The tubes may be purchased from stores that handle sports equipment; these can then be cut into thirds.

Activities with Scarves: Scarves can teach a child to be more aware of spatial relationships, and to discriminate between colors and shapes while following and leading individuals. Sequencing may also be introduced. Each child is permitted to freely explore forms of movement patterns, bilateral and unilateral, without restrictions or failure. The children are asked to:

1. Identify the color, shape, or number of sides of the scarf.

2. Hold the scarf in one's left or right hand.

3. Make the scarf go up, down, or around.

4. Throw the scarf in the air and catch it.

5. Find a partner and hold two scarves between the two (Each is to sense or feel the movement of the one chosen as the leader.)

Ropes, string, or elastic may also be used.

Yarn Activities: By using various lengths of yarn, the child has an opportunity to improve in the areas of spatial relationships, directionality, laterality, and body image while mirroring the leader. This activity can increase the child's understanding of words such as *in*, *out*, *above*, *below*, or *around*. Also, nonverbal commands may be used. Children may step on a line or circle made from yarn in order to gain the concept of a line or circle. Locomotor activities such as hopping, jumping, running, etc. may be performed along the various shapes. Two pieces of yarn are tied together. As the yarn is distributed to the children, they are asked to identify the color of the yarn. The long and short ends of the yarn are also located. Then the yarn is placed on the floor—in the shape of a mountain, for example. At first the children are asked to move only the feet;

as they step in and out and forward and backward. Then arm movements are added to the foot motions. This concept may also be used as a lead-in activity prior to teaching jumping jacks, as a race or game, or a rhythm activity. This can lead into a nonverbal activity with the children acting as leaders. The yarn and scarves may be used at the same time.*

Bamboo Poles: Several poles may be placed in lines on the floor. The students are lined up facing the poles. Any locomotor activity may be performed over or under the poles. One pole might be held up high and the next pole lowered; then the child is instructed to go around the obstacles. Also, sequencing may be introduced. Instructions should be simple at first and then slowly progress to a more difficult level. These instructions, first written on cards or on a board, might include:

1. Hop over the first pole.
2. Turn and jump over the second pole.
3. Crab walk over the third pole.

Later, only verbal cues may be given. For the older and more coordinated students, the poles may be laid apart on the floor and students are in a line facing the side of the poles. They are told to take one step between the poles and then to step on the outside. The words "in-in-out" are repeated in unison so that the students begin to feel the rhythm. As the students improve their timing and rhythm, two are selected to operate the poles in time to the rhythmetical chant "in-in-out."

Balloon Activities: Balloons are very motivating to children and provide an excellent inexpensive teaching aid. All is needed is your imagination. These activities might include the following:

1. Have a race to see who can keep the balloon in the air the longest period of time.
2. Have the students walk, jump, or hop with the balloon held between the legs.
3. Place the balloon between two students and have them walk forward, backward, or side-

ways.

4. Have students kick or push a balloon around an obstacle course.

5. Have students push a balloon with their nose to a designated space for a relay race.

6. Have the students carry an empty balloon to a specific spot, then blow it up and pop it.

7. Use balloons for balls in relay and circle games.

Chair Acivities: The students are given commands in the use of individual chairs in the classroom. These commands are as follows:

1. Stand up, sit down (repeat).
2. Run around the chair.
3. Run backwards around the chair.
4. Skip, hop, or jump around the chair.
5. Crawl under or through the chair.
6. Pick chair up and hold in front of body.
7. Hold chair over head, lower, and raise again.
8. Step up and down on the chair.
9. Place different body parts on the chair. For example: place your right hand under the chair and your feet on the seat of the chair.
10. Play "Musical Chairs."
11. Use chairs for an obstacle course.

With rows of chairs, the children might:

1. Fill chairs with students. On command each student moves forward one chair, with the person in the first chair moving to the rear.

2. Move according to the number of the activity. For example: (1) move to the right; (2) move to the left; (3) move forward; (4) move backward.

3. Make each line a team, then give some of the above commands and the first row to reseat all its team members is the winner.

100 Ways to Get There: A rope is layed on the floor in a straight line. The children are told to pretend that the rope is a road down which they will move. Each child must move down the road in a different way than the person in front of him. Encourage the children to be creative and see how many different ways they can move down the road. Examples of different movements are:

1. Walking
2. Skipping
3. Hopping
4. Jumping
5. Moving sideways and backwards
6. Doing animal walks

References

Boyer, Madeline Haas. *The Teaching of Elementary School Physical Education:* New York. J. Lowell Pratt and Co., 1965.

Cratty, Bryant J. *Learning and Playing.* Freeport, New York: Educational Activities, 1968.

Davis, Ernie. Material from a special workshop presented at the Fifth Annual Mid-Winter Conference (Ft. Worth, Texas, Fall, 1962).

Fait, Hollis F. *Special Physical Education.* Philadelphia: Saunders, 1966.

Hayden, Frank J. *Physical Fitness for the Mentally Retarded.* Ontario, Canada: University of Western Ontario, 1964.

Kirchner, Glenn. *Physical Education for Elementary Children.* Dubuque, Iowa: Wm. C. Brown, 1966.

Schurr, Evelyn L. *Movement Experiences for Children.* New York: Appleton-Century-Crofts., 1967.

Texas Department of Mental Health and Mental Retardation. *Recreation and Physical Education Guide* (Austin, Texas, 1973).